Fantastic

Volume 1

FAMILY NIGHTS!

SUSAN LUKE

*To my husband, Monty, and my children, Chris, Kim, Corinne,
Karalyn, Ammon, and Jeffe, whom I dearly love.*

Covenant Communications, Inc.
American Fork, Utah

Printed in the United States of America
First Printing: April 1993
93 94 95 96 97   10 9 8 7 6 5 4 3 2

Fantastic Family Nights
ISBN 1-55503-520-5
Library of Congress Catalog Card Number: 92-75978

Cover Illustration: Val Bagley
Cover Design: Amy A. Floyd

Covenant
Communications, Inc.

LESSONS
&
ACTIVITIES

"Our Family Record"

"Write the things which thou hast seen." Revelation 1:19

OBJECT:

To help family members learn the importance of keeping a family record.

PREPARATION:

1. Obtain a three-ring binder or other notebook to keep your family record in.

2. Gather a few family photos that you want to include in your family record.

3. Copy the appropriate pages from this book and punch the proper number of holes in them to fit in the binder you have obtained. Optional: To keep the pages in good condition, you may want to purchase clear vinyl sheet protectors to put them in. Do not punch holes in pages you plan to put in vinyl protectors.

4. Copy extra "Weekly Journal," "Family Home Evening," and "Family Photo" sheets for future use (punch holes in them and store in the binder).

5. Prayerfully study 3 Nephi 23:6-14.

SUGGESTED SONG:

"Genealogy—I Am Doing It," Children's Songbook, p. 94.

LESSON:

Have a fun evening sharing family memories and making a record of them. Spend some time talking about the importance of record keeping and then have an enjoyable time putting together your own family record.

Explain that all through the scriptures, the prophets were commanded to keep records of their people. There are several reasons to keep records. In 1 Nephi 1:3, Nephi states the following: "And I know that the record which I make is true: and I make it with mine own hand; and I make it according to my knowledge." No one else can keep a more accurate record of our families than we can. Sometimes facts can become distorted as they pass from one generation to another. This won't happen if we keep accurate records now.

The Lord commanded Abraham to write "for the benefit of my posterity that shall come after me." (Abraham 1:31.) Future generations can learn from our records just as we learn from past records.

Point out things we can learn from our own family histories. It's always fun to read about previously recorded events to see how our lives have progressed. Sometimes we may have to write about sad or discouraging things. After the sad events have passed, however, we can read about those events, recognize the blessings Heavenly Father has given to us, and be grateful for them. We can become closer as families when we gather around and spend time reading and remembering past events.

When Christ visited the Americas, he commanded that records should be kept. Relate the story found in 3 Nephi 23:6-14. Someday Jesus might ask us to bring forth our records. Will our records be accurate and complete?

ACTIVITY:

Spend time putting together a family record.

As a regular part of future family home evenings, allow a little time to record the events of the previous week. Include a brief record of your family home evenings. You may want to designate one family member (like King Benjamin did to Mosiah) and "give him charge concerning the records." Give that person the responsibility for a month or more and then give the charge to someone else.

Handy Hint #1

To create more family involvement, let your children help prepare the visual aids. Perhaps they could help cut, color, glue, or laminate. Better yet, if you have children who are old enough to handle it, give them the book and have them prepare and give a lesson all by themselves!

Our Family Record

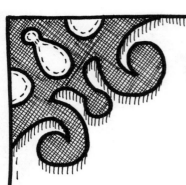

FAMILY PHOTOS

OUR TALENTS

OUR WORK

OUR VACATIONS

_____

_____

_____

_____

_____

_____

_____

_____

_____

_____

_____

_____

_____

_____

_____

_____

_____

_____

_____

_____

_____

_____

Our Family Journal
for the week of:

Family Home Evening

Date: _____

Opening Song: _____

Opening Prayer: _____

Family Business: _____

_____

_____

_____

_____

The lesson was given by: _____

The lesson topic was: _____

_____

_____

Other family members who participated were:

_____

_____

_____

Game or activity: _____

_____

_____

Closing Prayer: _____

Treat: _____

"Love at Home"

"Be ye kind one to another." Ephesians 4:32

OBJECT:

To learn how to better appreciate the ones we love.

PREPARATION:

1. Copy, color, cut, and laminate the "Sacrifices" game cards.

2. Copy, color, cut, assemble, and laminate crown.

3. Make a copy of "My family loves me because . . ." for each family member.

4. Prayerfully study the story of Abraham and Isaac (Genesis 22).

SUGGESTED SONG:

"Love at Home," Hymnbook, p. 294.

LESSON:

Begin with the game "Sacrifices." Follow the directions given on the following page. When finished, spend some time discussing which things were chosen as the most important. Ask, how should we treat these things? How much time should we devote to them? Explain that if Heavenly Father and our families are most important to us, we should treat them with love and respect by putting them first.

Share the story of Abraham and Isaac.

Gather the family in a circle. Have someone begin by putting on the crown. While that person is wearing the crown, have family members take turns telling what they love about him or her. Have someone record what is said on the "My family loves me because . . ." sheet. This sheet can be saved so that the individual can refer to it periodically. Continue until everyone has had a chance to wear the crown.

To promote further thoughtfulness, have family members draw names for secret pals and do special things for them during the coming week. If this is successful, redraw names at every family home evening for a while, allowing family members to share the special things that occurred during the week.

SACRIFICES

OBJECT: To learn what things are most important to us.*

HOW TO PLAY: Cut out cards and spread them out faceup. Take turns
choosing which card we could sacrifice if we had to.
Continue until only 3-5 cards remain.

* Sometimes we get caught up in everyday living and forget what is really
important to us. We treat our friends with more respect than we treat
our families, we place more importance on schoolwork or a job than we do
on our families, or we spend more time thinking about food or money than
we do our own families. Hopefully this game will help us realize what is
"most" important to us.

Aunts, Uncles,
Cousins

COMPUTERS

DENTISTS

FOOD

MONEY

 Cars,
Planes,
& Trains

TELEPHONES

BROTHERS
&
SISTERS

DOCTORS

Personal
Talents

FRIENDS

SCHOOL

Television

TOYS

BOOKS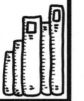

MY FAMILY LOVES ME BECAUSE...

_____
_____
_____
_____
_____
_____
_____
_____
_____
_____
_____
_____
_____
_____
_____
_____
_____
_____
_____
_____
_____
_____
_____
_____

DATE _____

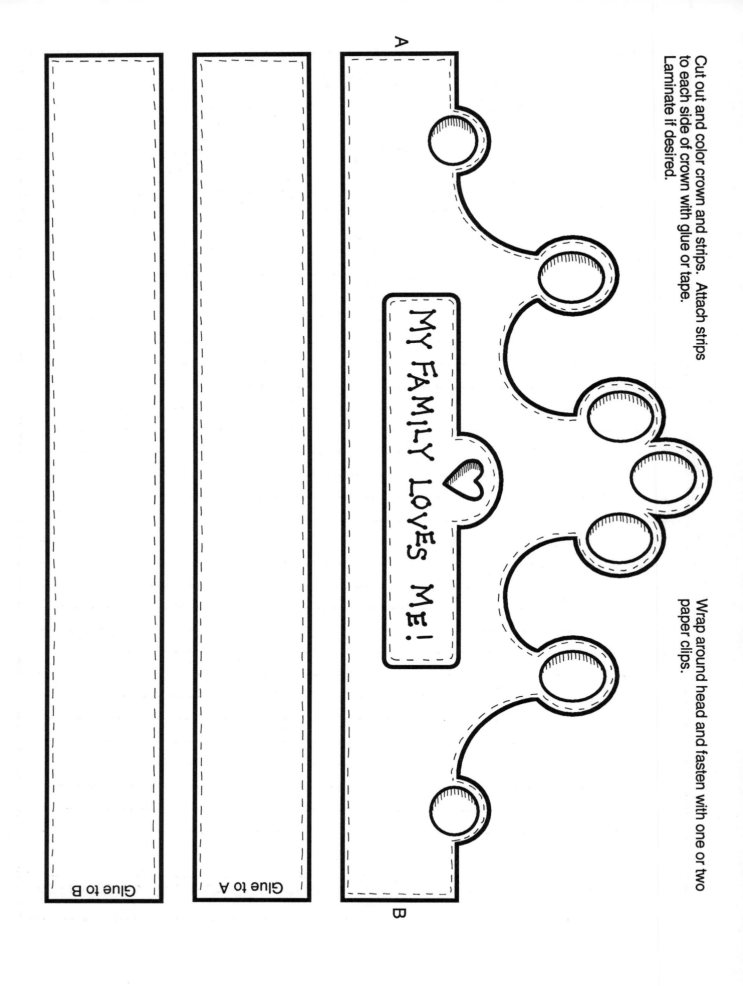

Cut out and color crown and strips. Attach strips
to each side of crown with glue or tape.
Laminate if desired.

Wrap around head and fasten with one or two
paper clips.

A

MY FAMILY LOVES ME!

B

Glue to A

Glue to B

3

"Pure Thoughts"

"Let virtue garnish thy thoughts unceasingly." D&C 121:45

OBJECT:

To help family members realize the importance of pure thoughts.

PREPARATION:

1. Prepare visual aids by following the directions on page 25.

2. Gather a clear quart jar, food coloring, bleach, and white vinegar.

3. Assign the following scriptures:

Leviticus 19:11
D&C 42:20

SUGGESTED SONG:

"I'm Trying to Be Like Jesus," Children's Songbook, p. 78.

LESSON:

Fill a quart jar $2/3$ full with water. Tape "The Right Way" sign to the back of the outside of the jar (so you can see through the water and read it). Explain that when your mind is full of pure thoughts you can see the "right way" easily. If you fill your mind with the wrong thoughts, the "right way" is harder to see. (Add a couple of drops of food coloring and stir.) Spend some time talking about why the wrong thoughts would make it harder to do what Heavenly Father wants us to do. Now explain that we can counteract bad thoughts by replacing them with good thoughts. (Pour a little bit of bleach and a little bit of white vinegar into the jar and stir.) The water turns clear again, making the "right way" easier to see. (Experiment before the lesson to determine how much of each to pour in.) Explain that we need to be careful what kind of thoughts we put into our minds. Just like the food coloring in the water, we might be able to counteract bad thoughts with good thoughts (bleach and vinegar), but it takes a great deal of effort to push them out of our minds.

Ask if it's possible to do something without thinking about it first. All actions begin as thoughts. If we strive to "let virtue garnish our thoughts unceasingly," then all of our actions will be pleasing to Heavenly Father.

STORY:

Tell the following story using the visual aids.

Sarah was a pleasant young girl who did many good things. She said her prayers and read her scriptures every day. She paid an honest tithe and obeyed her parents. She always worked hard to help around the house. Sarah always tried to fill her mind with pleasant thoughts.

One day her mom gave her permission to go the mall with her friends. Sarah and her friends walked around the mall for a while and decided to see a newly released movie. All of her friends said that the movie would be really good. They bought their tickets and went inside and sat down. As they were watching the movie, Sarah noticed that the kids in the movie wore expensive designer clothes. She looked over at her friends and noticed that many of them wore the same kind of expensive clothing. Sarah felt embarrassed and put her feet under her chair as she remembered that her shoes were hand-me-downs from an older cousin.

As she watched the movie, she noticed that the kids told some unclean jokes and swore occasionally. This made her feel uncomfortable, but she didn't think hearing those things would really hurt her. She didn't realize that her good thoughts were slowly being replaced by bad thoughts.

When they got out of the movie, they walked around the mall again. They talked about the movie and how cool the kids in the movie were. They had so many material things. All of their clothes were awesome. Sarah kept thinking how great it would be to have something expensive, too. She told her friends how she wished she could have expensive things like the kids in the movie, but could never afford them. One of her friends suggested stealing something expensive from a store. Sarah knew that stealing was wrong but she wanted to fit in so badly that she began to consider stealing.

She looked around for a while and found something that she really liked. Her heart started to beat faster and faster. She was so nervous! She didn't realize that the feeling she had came from the Holy Ghost, who was trying to warn her not to steal. She looked around to be sure no one was watching and slipped something into her purse.

When she got home, Sarah felt awful about what she had done. Her mind had been completely filled with bad thoughts. She had let thoughts of jealousy and greed control her actions. She had completely ignored the promptings of the Holy Ghost. She needed to do something to correct the mistake she had made. She found her scriptures and started reading. She read Leviticus 19:11 and D&C 42:20. (Have someone read these scriptures aloud.) She knelt down and prayed to her Heavenly Father for forgiveness. When she finished, she felt that she needed to tell her parents what she had done. They talked things over and decided that she needed to return the thing she had stolen to the store and apologize to the owner. When she went back to the store, Sarah also offered free help to the store owner to make up for what she had done. Sarah learned a hard lesson about the power of thoughts and vowed always to keep good thoughts in her mind.

18

ACTIVITY:

Take turns guessing each other's thoughts. Start by thinking of something good and then give clues to family members so they can try to guess what you are thinking. Begin with general clues, then get more specific. For example, your thought might be "the temple." Your clues might be: "It's a kind of building. There are several of them all over the world. Some are bigger than others. Some are older than others. One took over forty years to build. It's a sacred place, etc."

The following pages offer possible words and clues. You will be able to think of many more.

Handy Hint #2

After teaching a lesson, place all of the visual aids along with the lesson into a manila envelope. Label each lesson with a name and a date (see example below). Store the manila envelopes neatly in a cardboard box or file. When you need to use the lesson or visual aids again, you will know exactly where to find them!

"Pure Thoughts"

Contents:
Lesson
Story with visual aids
"The Right Way" label
Thought cards

Date Given: _____
Comments: _____
_____
_____
_____

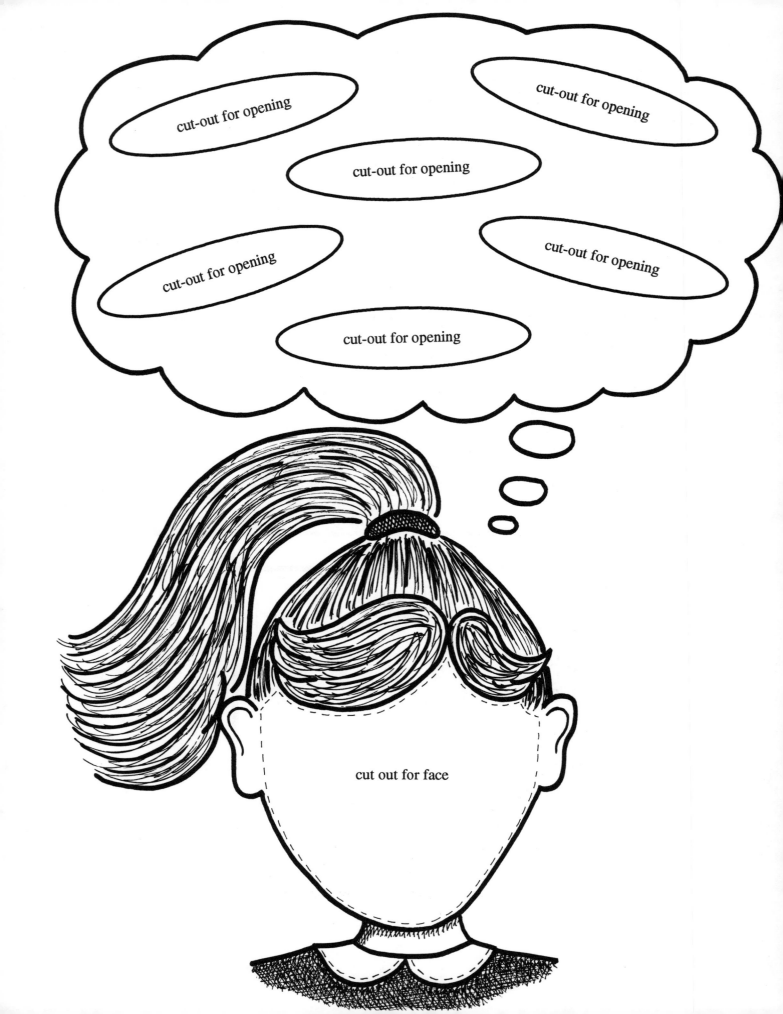

Heavenly Father

Prayer

Honesty

Helping Others

Family

Scriptures

Unclean Jokes

Prayer

Swear Words

Family

Helping Others

Unclean Movies

Unclean Jokes

Greed

Swear Words

Stealing

Jealousy

Unclean Movies

The Golden Plates

1. Old
2. Shiny
3. Something to write on

Baptism

1. A commandment
2. Usually happens in youth
3. Immersion

Holy Ghost

1. Makes us feel good
2. Special gift
3. Third member of the Godhead

Temples

1. Buildings
2. Beautiful
3. Spires

Primary

1. Organization
2. Sing songs
3. Young children

Bishop

1. Church calling
2. Friendly person
3. Leader of ward

Testimony

1. Personal
2. Good feeling inside
3. Knowledge of the truth

Brigham Young

1. Leader
2. Prophet
3. Pioneers

Prophet

1. Person
2. Called of God
3. Leads our church

Family

1. Love
2. Group
3. Eternal

Missionary

1. Person
2. Dedicated
3. Teaches the gospel

Articles of Faith

1. Words
2. Gospel
3. Thirteen

Sacrament Meeting

1. Activity
2. Sunday
3. Talks or testimonies

Tithing

1. Commandment
2. Blessings
3. One-tenth

How to Prepare Visual Aids

Cut out "The Right Way" label and tape it to the outside of a quart jar, toward the bottom so that you can see it through the glass. Fill the jar $\frac{1}{2}$ full with water. Set aside.

Color and cut out the remaining pages of visual aids. Cut openings on the cover page as directed. Lay the first page of words behind the cover page and line it up so you can read the words easily through each opening. Mark around the edges lightly with a pencil so you will know where to cut. Do the same with the remaining pages. Trim the edges so that the page will fit easily into a clear sheet protector. Now trim the remaining pages so they will fit in the same sheet protector behind the cover page.

As you tell the story, pull one page out at a time from behind the cover page and replace it in the back. (During the story, you will display page 1, then page 2, then page 3, and then page 1 again.) Practice the story with the visual aids before family home evening.

"Building a House of God"

"Prepare every needful thing; and establish . . . a house of God." D&C 88:119

OBJECT:

To help family members learn how to help make their home a house of God.

PREPARATION:

1. Copy, color, cut, and laminate the visual aids.

2. Assign the following scriptures (or mark them for your own reference):

D&C 88:119-120	3 Nephi 18:21
2 Nephi 32:9	3 Nephi 13:16-18
Ether 12:28-30	D&C 19:23
D&C 90:15	Mosiah 2:41
D&C 90:18	D&C 132:8

3. Get tape or "Fun-tack" for displaying the visual aids.

4. Prayerfully study the parable of the wise man and the foolish man. (See Matthew 7:24-27.)

SUGGESTED SONG:

"The Wise Man and the Foolish Man," Children's Songbook, p. 281.

LESSON:

Begin by telling the parable of the wise man and the foolish man. Ask if anyone knows the meaning of the parable. Explain that the rock symbolizes the gospel of Jesus Christ. If we have the gospel as a foundation in our lives, then we will be able to stand in times of adversity and not fall, just as the wise man's house withstood the rain and floods. Ask, "What should we do to make the gospel a foundation for our 'house.'" Display the outline of the house while someone reads D&C 88:119-120.

Put the house part labeled "prayer" in its proper place on the house. Ask, "How can we have a house of prayer." (Answers: By having family prayers and personal prayers.) Have the assigned persons read 3 Nephi 18:21 and 2 Nephi 32:9 to learn what the scriptures say about prayer.

Now put the house part labeled "fasting" in its proper place. Ask, "How can we have a house of fasting?" (By observing Fast Sunday, bearing our testimonies, and paying fast offerings.) To learn the proper way of fasting, have someone read 3 Nephi 13:16-18.

Next is the label of "faith." Ask, "How can we have a house of faith?" (Answers: By praying, attending church, and studying the scriptures.) To learn the blessings of faith, have someone read Ether 12:28-30.

Now add "learning." Ask, "How can we have a house of learning?" (By reading good books, having family home evenings, and studying scriptures.) The scriptures say we should not only learn of Christ, but of languages, tongues, and people. Have someone read D&C 19:23 and D&C 90:15.

Next is the label of "glory." The dictionary defines "glory" as "the splendor and perfect happiness of heaven." Ask. "How can we achieve that kind of happiness in our own homes?" (Answer: By living the commandments of Heavenly Father.) Have someone read Mosiah 2:41 to learn the blessings of living the commandments.

Now add the label of "order." Ask, "How can we achieve order in our home?" (Answers: By fulfilling individual responsibilities, following rules or guidelines, and showing respect for each other.) The scriptures tell us that our homes should be clean and free of confusion (both physically and spiritually).

Have someone read D&C 90:18 and D&C 132:8.

Finally, add the label of "God." Ask, "How can we have a house of God?" (Answers: By showing kindness, patience, love, and respect for one another.) In the Book of Mormon we learn that when the people had a love for God, there was no contention in the land (4 Nephi 1:15). If our hearts are filled with the love of God, then our homes will have less contention and more peace and happiness.

Conclude by reading D&C 124:55. Display the "house" during the week and challenge every family member to strive to establish a "house of God."

27

GOD

ORDER

FASTING

LEARNING

FAITH

GLORY

PRAYER

Cut apart and position each part (i.e., God, Order, Learning) on the house outline as you ask the questions listed in the "House of God" lesson.

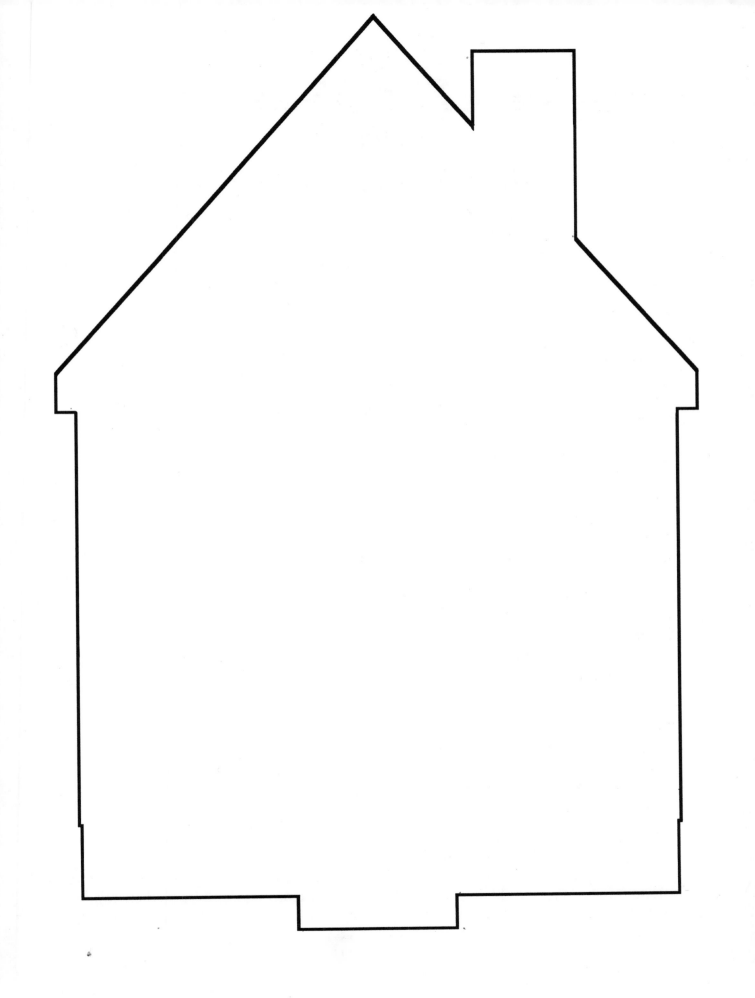

"Fun With Music"

"If thou art merry, praise the Lord with singing, with music, with dancing, and with a prayer of praise and thanksgiving." D&C 136:28

OBJECT:

To help family members understand the power and influence of music, and the importance of music in worshiping our Heavenly Father.

PREPARATION:

1. Copy, color, cut, and laminate the visual aids. Glue a wooden stick to the back of each one.

2. Make a copy of the crossword puzzle for each family member.

3. Gather supplies for the homemade instruments mentioned in the lesson. (Optional.)

4. Gather pens or pencils for everyone.

5. Gather a variety of types of music to play on a cassette or compact disk player, or sheet music to play on the piano.

SUGGESTED SONG:

"Lift Up Your Voice and Sing," Children's Songbook, p. 252.

EXPERIMENT:

Have all the members of your family close their eyes while you play several different kinds of music. Let family members explain how each song makes them feel. Try to play a variety of music that makes them feel happy, sad, energetic, angry, etc.

LESSON:

Begin by explaining that music is an important part of worship to our Heavenly Father. Read 1 Nephi 1:8: "He saw the heavens open, and he thought he saw God sitting upon his throne, surrounded with numberless concourses of angels in the attitude of singing and praising their God." Explain that the scriptures tell us that angelic choirs sang in the preexistence: "The morning stars sang together, and all the sons of God shouted for joy." (Job 38:7) Heavenly hosts also announced the birth of our Savior: "Glory to God in the highest, and on earth peace, good will toward men." (Luke 2:14) We read all through Psalms that we should sing for joy, strength, and thankfulness. We should sing praise to God's righteousness, power, and mercy. We should sing in honor of God's name. We should sing with understanding. We should praise the Lord with song and instrument. We should sing because of our blessings. We should sing to "declare among the people his doings." (Psalms 9:11.) To further understand the importance of singing, have a family member read Psalms 150:1-6.

Point out that music can have a powerful influence on us. As we learned in the beginning experiment, some music can put us in happy, energetic moods, while other music makes us feel calm and peaceful inside. Some music can even make us feel sad or depressed, and certain music can have a bad influence and direct our thoughts in the wrong direction.

Ask family members if they have ever had a song "stuck" in their head while the tune and lyrics played repeatedly in their minds. Ask, "What happens if the song is not wholesome or uplifting?" Through bad music, Satan can subtly place bad thoughts in our minds—thoughts we may act upon some day. However, if a song is wholesome and uplifting, it can make us feel good inside and influence our thoughts in a way that would be pleasing to our Heavenly Father. A good song can be a tool to help us get through a tough situation by reminding us of wholesome things. For instance, ask family members, "How could you do something wrong when the words to, 'I Am a Child of God,' are going through your head?"

Allow family members time to discuss any personal experiences they have had with the influence of music, both good or bad.

Encourage family members to choose their music wisely so that its influence will be uplifting and pleasing to Heavenly Father.

ACTIVITIES:

Pass out the crossword puzzles and allow time to complete them. Have older family members help younger ones.

After the puzzles are completed, lead the family in their favorite songs. Hold up the visual aids one at a time during the songs, alternating the visual aids as many times as you like during each song. Take turns being the "leader" of the visual aids. Have fun humming one line, whistling the next, singing fast, then singing slowly, etc. If you have musically talented family members, they could provide accompaniment. If you don't have any "trained" musicians, try making your own instruments (described below) or just sing acappela.

OPTIONAL FUN:

Your family may want to be creative and make their own musical instruments to use during their singing time such as the following:

• An oatmeal box or gallon can used as a drum.

• Cooking lids used as cymbals.

• A spoon grazed across a washboard or a dowel grazed across a can with ridges.

• A small glass jar filled with popcorn or beans used as a shaker.

• A shoebox with rubber bands around it to snap.

• Blocks of wood covered with sandpaper to rub together.

• Jingle bells attached to your fingers with elastic.

"Fun With Music"

ACROSS

1. ___ is for courage. . .
5. Has given me an _____ home. . .
7. I ____ the Lord provides a way; he wants me to obey.
9. You have a work that __ other can do.
11. Though ____ to you this journey may appear. . .
12. For some must ____ and some must pull. . .
14. They are __ good to me.
15. The ____ man built his house upon the rock.
16. I want to be ____ to everyone.
22. Keep the _____.
24. Jesus wants __ for a sunbeam.
26. I'll obey his living prophets in all they ___.
28. Quickly I'll ____.
29. I can do and say _____ things each day.
30. I often __ walking.
32. Long ago their _____ came from far across the sea. . .
34. Whenever I feel the ____ on my face. . .
35. Peace and _____ here abide.

DOWN

1. _____ beamed the sun above.
2. ____ to do right.
3. The Spirit of God like a ____ is burning.
4. If you _____ to meet a frown. . .
6. I'll prepare myself while I am _____.
8. I _____ when he comes again. . .
10. I hear the words she _____ when she bows her head to pray.
13. As it _____ down the hill.
15. Teach me to ____ in the light of his love.
17. To guide us in these latter ____.
18. We'll sing and we'll shout with the _____ of heaven.
19. ____ my hands and jump for joy.
20. The golden plates lay _____. . .
21. We are as the armies of _____.
22. _____ to serve.
23. _____ children sang as they walked.
25. Saturday is a special ___.
27. When upon life's billows ___ are tempest tossed.
30. Be _____ and loving in deed and in thought . . .
31. I kneel to ____ every day.
32. _____ is knowing the sun will rise. . .
33. Spring ___ brought me such a nice surprise.

CROSSWORD PUZZLE ANSWERS

ANSWERS ACROSS	ANSWERS DOWN
1. RED	1. RADIANT
5. EARTHLY	2. DARE
7. KNOW	3. FIRE
9. NO	4. CHANCE
11. HARD	6. YOUNG
12. PUSH	8. WONDER
14. SO	10. WHISPERS
15. WISE	13. HURRIED
16. KIND	15. WALK
22. COMMANDMENTS	17. DAYS
24. ME	18. ARMIES
26. SAY	19. CLAP
28. OBEY	20. HIDDEN
29. HAPPY	21. HELAMAN
30. GO	22. CALLED
32. FATHERS	23. PIONEER
34. RAIN	25. DAY
35. PLENTY	27. YOU
	30 GENTLE
	31. PRAY
	32. FAITH
	33. HAS

"Natural Consequences"

"Remember that ye are free to act for yourselves--to choose the way of everlasting death or the way of eternal life." 2 Nephi 10:23

OBJECT:

To help family members realize that even though we can choose our actions, we cannot choose the consequences that follow.

PREPARATION:

1. Copy game pages, trim edge of pages as indicated, overlap and glue them together. Color, trim, and laminate.

2. Copy, cut, and laminate game cards.

3. Copy, cut, color, laminate, and assemble spinner as directed.

4. Gather small objects or buttons to be used as markers for the game.

5. Gather various items needed for the demonstration (listed below).

6. Prayerfully study the story of Laman and Lemuel and the Liahona (1 Nephi 18:5-22).

SUGGESTED SONG:

"Dare to Do Right," Children's Songbook, p. 158.

LESSON:

Begin by presenting various objects to the family to demonstrate natural consequences. For example:

1. Blow up a balloon and let the air out so it will fly around the room.

2. Blow up a balloon and pop it with a pin.

3. Push "play" on a tape player and listen to the sounds.

4. Flip the switch on the TV to turn it on.

5. Turn the volume control up for more sound.

6. Hold a book in the air and drop it.

7. Stretch a rubber band and let it go.

Use the examples listed or come up with your own object lessons. Explain that every action has a consequence, good or bad. When we came to this earth, we were given free agency. We can choose to take any action, but we can't choose the consequences of our actions.

Relate the scripture story of Laman and Lemuel. Talk about the consequences that followed the different actions. For example, the Liahona "did cease to work" when Laman and Lemuel tied up Nephi. They didn't know which way to steer the ship. When they let Nephi loose, the Liahona began to work again. Also, when Nephi prayed to Heavenly Father, the winds and storm ceased.

GAME:

Play the game of "Natural Consequences."

SUGGESTED GUIDELINES:

After deciding who goes first, take turns spinning the spinner and moving the appropriate number of spaces.

If you land on a "roadblock" space, collect a card and save it for when you land on a "detour" space. This will prevent you from going off the straight and narrow path. Once you have used the "roadblock" card, return it to the pile.

If you land on a "detour" space, move to the first space on the "detour" and draw a "consequence" card. Follow the directions on the card. On your next turn, move to the next space (don't spin the spinner), draw a "consequence" card and follow the directions on the card. On your next turn, do the same. On your next turn, spin the spinner and move the appropriate number of spaces.

If you a draw a "consequence" card that tells you to move ahead to the next "positive" space, skip the rest of the "detour" spaces and get back on the straight and narrow path.

The first one to reach the "celestial kingdom" is the winner!

Handy Hint #3

If your younger children have a problem with reverence during family home evening, try giving each family member a special place to sit. Ways of marking these special places include a special "Family Home Evening Blanket," individualized carpet squares, fabric name tags placed on the furniture, etc. Use these things only for family home evening.

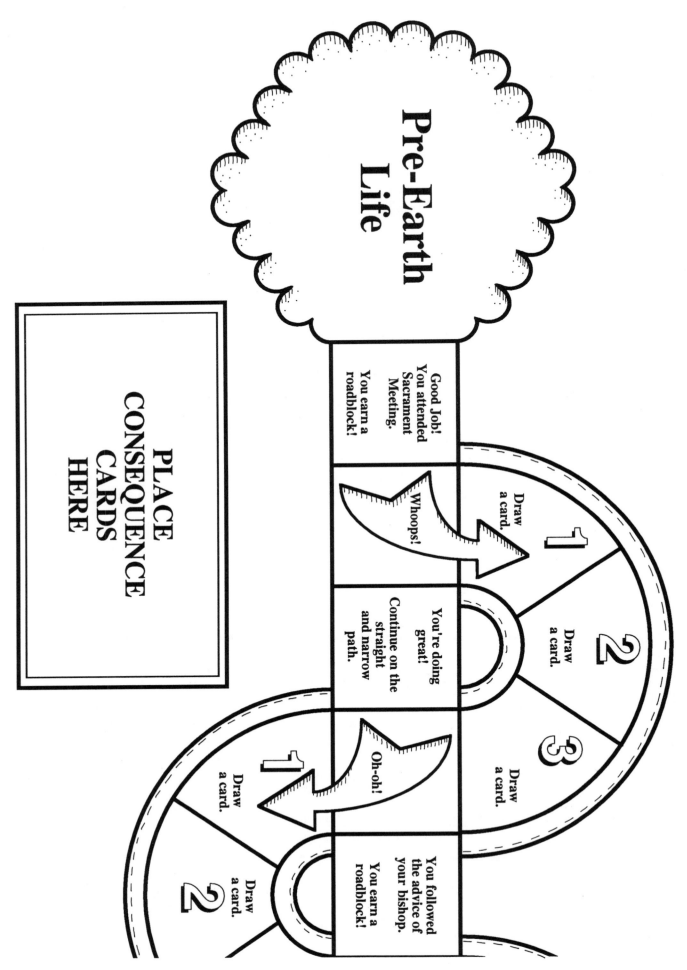

Pre-Earth Life

PLACE CONSEQUENCE CARDS HERE

Good Job! You attended Sacrament Meeting.

You earn a roadblock!

Draw a card.

Whoops!

1

2

3

Draw a card.

Draw a card.

You're doing great! Continue on the straight and narrow path.

Oh-oh!

1

Draw a card.

You followed the advice of your bishop.

You earn a roadblock!

2

Draw a card.

Trim this edge and overlap onto edge A.

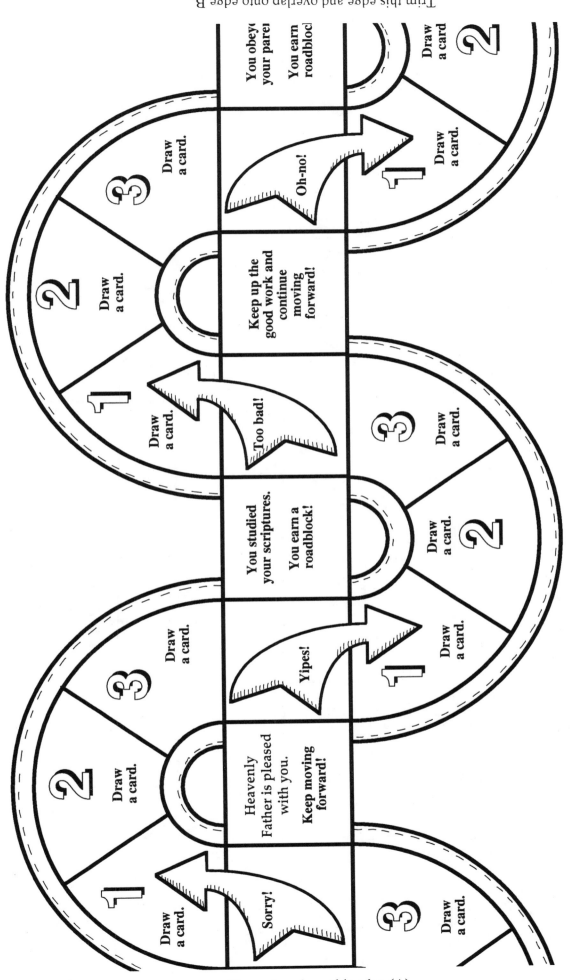

You obey your pare

You earn roadbloc

Draw a card.

2

3

Draw a card.

Oh-no!

1

Draw a card.

2

Draw a card.

Keep up the good work and continue moving forward!

1

Draw a card.

Too bad!

3

Draw a card.

You studied your scriptures.

You earn a roadblock!

2

Draw a card.

Draw a card.

Yipes!

1

Draw a card.

3

Draw a card.

2

Draw a card.

Heavenly Father is pleased with you.

Keep moving forward!

1

Draw a card.

Sorry!

3

Draw a card.

Place glue along this edge (A).

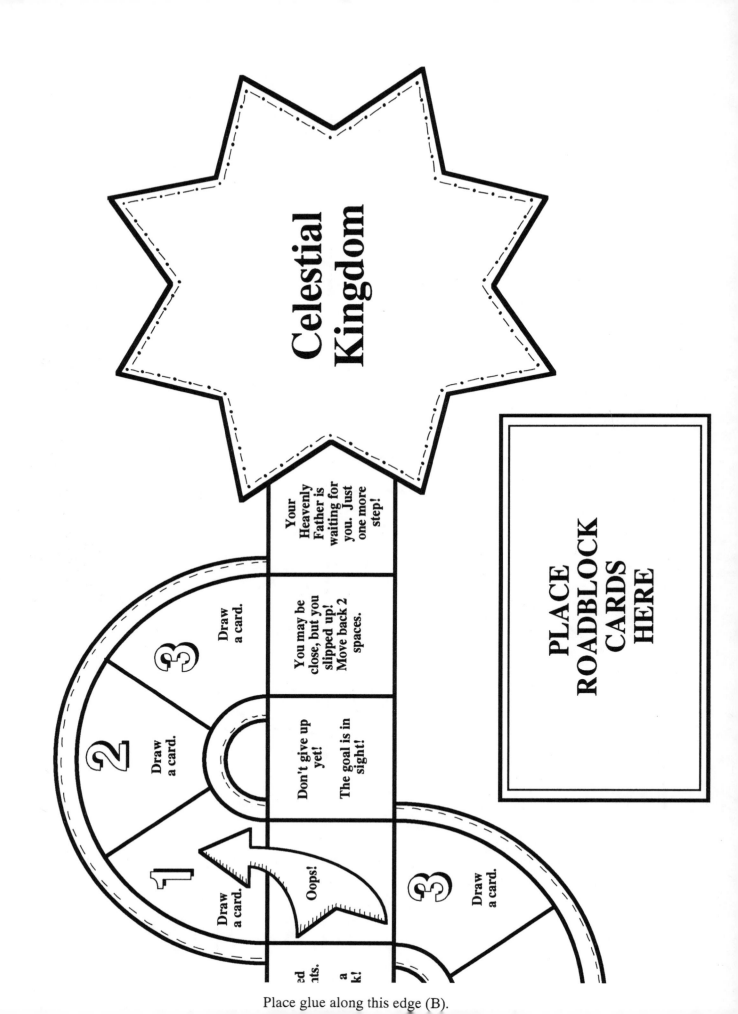

Celestial Kingdom

Your Heavenly Father is waiting for you. Just one more step!

You may be close, but you slipped up! Move back 2 spaces.

Don't give up yet! The goal is in sight!

Draw a card.

③

②

Draw a card.

①

Oops!

③

Draw a card.

PLACE ROADBLOCK CARDS HERE

Place glue along this edge (B).

Remove page from book and glue securely to lightweight cardboard or posterboard. Trim edges around spinner base and arrow. Color and laminate the pieces if you desire. Punch a small hole in the center of the base and the arrow. Fasten the arrow to the base with a paper brad leaving it a little loose so that it will spin freely.

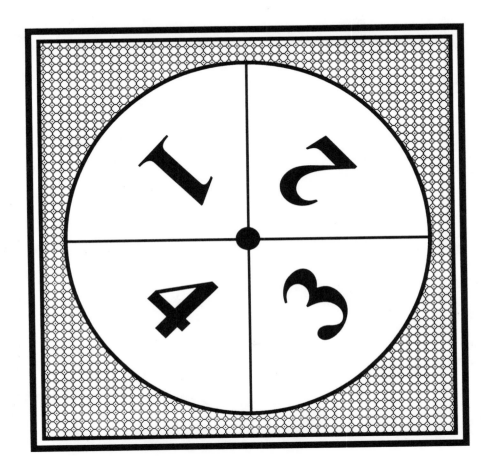

Explain the proper steps of repentance.

Name four things you can do to keep the Sabbath Day holy.

Name four things you can do to please Heavenly Father.

What are some of the positive consequences of fasting?

What can happen when you spread a rumor about someone? Why is spreading rumors wrong?

Why is it important to obey the Word of Wisdom?

Name four things you can do to obey your parents.

What are some of the positive consequences of telling the truth?

What should you do if you take something that doesn't belong to you?

What does it mean to use the Lord's name in vain? Why is it wrong?

Recite the second article of faith. (Hint: Adam's transgression.)

What are some of the positive consequences of obeying the Word of Wisdom?

What are some of the negative consequences of smoking cigarettes?

What are some of the negative consequences of drinking alcohol?

What are some of the negative consequences of thinking impure thoughts?

What are some of the positive consequences of paying tithes?

After properly repenting and receiving forgiveness, does Heavenly Father remember your sins? (D&C 58:42)

What are some of the negative consequences of stealing?

What are some of the negative consequences of cheating?

What are some of the positive consequences of listening to the Holy Ghost?

What does it mean to repent? How many times can you repent in your life?

What are some of the negative consequences of telling a lie?

What are some of the negative consequences of showing your anger?

What are some of the positive consequences of having a cheerful attitude?

What are some of the negative consequences of breaking laws?

What are some of the negative consequences of disobeying traffic signals?

What are some of the positive consequences of going to bed on time?

What are some of the positive consequences for going to bed on time?

What are some of the negative consequences of being selfish?

What are some of the negative consequences of gossiping?

What are some of the positive consequences of having family prayer?

What are some of the positive consequences for doing your homework?

What are some of the negative consequences of complaining?

What are some of the negative consequences of dressing immodestly?

What are some of the positive consequences of personal prayer?

What are some of the positive consequences for attending school?

You're forgiven of your mistake! Move to the next "roadblock" space.

You're forgiven of your mistake! Move to the next "roadblock" space.

If you told a lie, what could you do to make it better?

What are some of the positive consequences of having regular family home evening?

You're forgiven of your mistake! Move to the next "roadblock" space.

You're forgiven of your mistake! Move to the next "roadblock" space.

Sing "I Need My Heavenly Father." Children's Songbook p.18

What are some of the positive consequences of attending church?

Sing "Dare to Do Right." Children's Songbook p. 158

You're forgiven of your mistake! Move to the next "roadblock" space.

Sing "I Am a Child of God." Children's Songbook p. 2

What are some of the positive consequences of reading scriptures?

ROADBLOCK CARDS

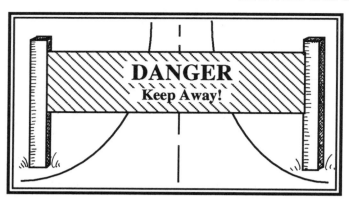
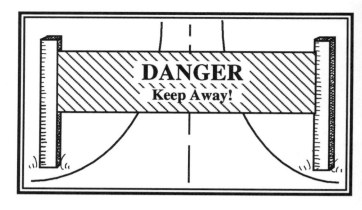

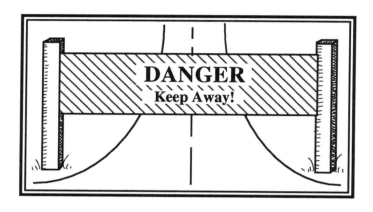
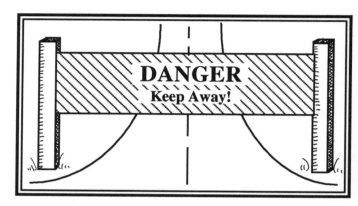

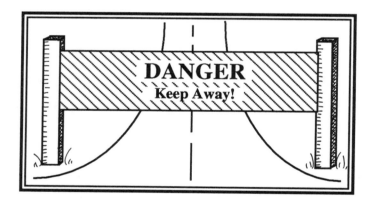
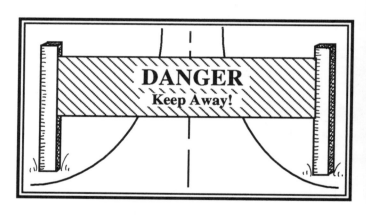

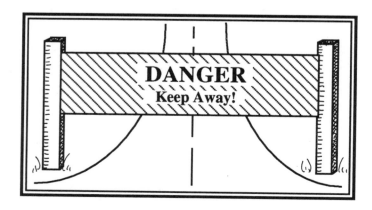
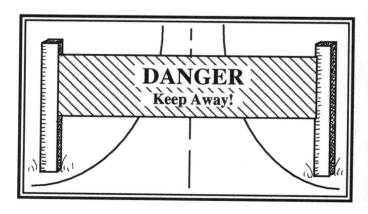

(Make 2 copies of this page)

"Avoiding Temptation"

"Watch and pray, that ye enter not into temptation." Matthew 26:41

SUBJECT:

To help teach family members how they can prepare themselves to avoid temptation.

PREPARATION:

1. Copy, color, cut, and laminate the visual aids.

2. Glue or tape a bamboo skewer to the back of each visual aid.

3. Gather tape and pliers.

4. Assign the following scriptures:

Ether 12:27
Corinthians 10:13

SUGGESTED SONG:

"Stand for the Right," Children's Songbook, p. 159.

LESSON:

Hold up the skewer with the picture of the girl on it for your family to see. Hold up the pliers and tell your family that the pliers represent temptation. Place the pliers on the skewer and break it. Explain that by ourselves we are easily "broken" by temptation. We can repent of our sins and be forgiven (tape the skewer back together), but Satan is clever and he knows our weaknesses. He will continue to attack us where we are weak unless we build up our weaknesses and turn them into strengths. (Have someone read Ether 12:27.) This scripture tells us that if we humble ourselves before Heavenly Father and have faith, then our weaknesses will become strengths. Add the other skewers (strengths) one at a time and talk about how each one is pleasing to Heavenly Father and, therefore, could help a person become stronger. Once all the skewers are all together, try again to break them with the pliers. It's much harder to be "broken" by temptation when we have so much help surrounding us.

Now ask someone to represent Satan and leave the room. Have this person stand behind a closed door (preferably one with a lock). Ask your family if Satan could get through the door without a key. He can't open locked doors. What happens, though, if we give in to a little temptation? It's as if we unlock the door (unlock the door). Then if we give in again, it's as if we are turning the knob (turn the knob). Soon giving in becomes easier and we open the door. Maybe just a crack to begin with (open it a crack). Before we know it, the door is wide open (open it all the way) and Satan can walk right in and destroy us. (Note: You may want to use an example of what Satan could tempt us with, such as drinking alcohol.) Even though we may say that we would never drink it, he could begin by having us watch beer commercials and becoming desensitized to them (unlock the door). Then we might start hanging out with other people who drink (turn the knob). Then we might take just a little taste (open the door just a crack), etc.

Explain that Heavenly Father has promised us that we will have the strength to resist any temptation. (Have someone read 1 Cor. 10:13.) Sometimes we may be in a situation that seems overwhelming to us. But if we remember Heavenly Father's promise, it will give us strength to overcome the temptation.

ACTIVITY:

One of the best ways to avoid temptation is to decide not to do certain things ahead of time while there is no pressure to do wrong. If the time comes when you are faced with temptation, you won't have to worry about making the wrong decision under pressure because you will have already decided (and promised to yourself) not to give in. Have each family member fill out a certificate and sign and date it (see page 51). These can be hung in their rooms as a reminder to resist temptations.

Handy Hint #4

Make family members feel special by spotlighting them individually. Choose a different family member each week. Talk about their accomplishments, talents, favorite things, etc. Serve their favorite dessert for the treat that night. You could even make them a special ribbon or award!

PRAYERS

REGULAR CHURCH ATTENDANCE

Scripture Study

HOLY GHOST

LOVE

FAITH

**SERVICE
TO
OTHERS**

I, _____ , want to be spiritually strong and avoid temptation at all times. Therefore, I am making a promise in advance to myself, my family, and my Heavenly Father to always . . .

_____
_____
_____
_____
_____
_____
_____
_____

Signed _____
Date _____

I, _____ , want to be spiritually strong and avoid temptation at all times. Therefore, I am making a promise in advance to myself, my family, and my Heavenly Father to always . . .

_____
_____
_____
_____
_____
_____
_____
_____

Signed _____
Date _____

"Good Fruits"

"Wherefore by their fruits ye shall know them." Matthew 7:20

OBJECT:

To help family members understand that all good things come from Heavenly Father and all bad things come from Satan.

PREPARATION:

1. Copy, color, cut, and laminate 2 trees, both pages of apples, and the labels.

2. Bake cookies according to directions.

3. Obtain tape or "Fun-tack."

4. Assign the following scriptures:

   Alma 5:40-41
   D&C 6:33

5. Prayerfully study Matthew 7:15-20.

SUGGESTED SONG:

"I Am Like a Star," Children's Songbook, p. 163.

LESSON:

Begin by displaying the two trees with the cookies on them. Ask which "cookie" tree the family members would like to have growing at their house. If your family is like most, they will choose the tree with the greater number of cookies on it. Now ask them if they would like to have a cookie from that tree. (At our house, my husband told the kids that the first one to eat their cookie would get to eat the rest of the cookies. They all ripped off the plastic and popped them into their mouths. A second later they were all running to the garbage to spit them out! Needless to say, they weren't very happy with us!)

After they all have drinks of water, ask them what they thought about the "fruit" of that tree. It looked good from the outside, but in reality, it tasted awful. Ask if they would like to taste the "fruit" of the other tree. (We had to assure our kids that we weren't going to trick them again!)

Ask, "Which tree had better fruit?" Place the "GOOD" label under the good tree and the "BAD" label under the bad tree. Read Matthew 7:15-20 and discuss it with your family. Remind them that the cookies all looked good from the outside, but some of them were "wolves in sheep's clothing." To help them further understand, have someone read Alma 5:40. If good is from God, and evil is from the devil, then one tree is from God, and one is from devil. When we allow ourselves to be contentious, selfish, jealous, etc., we, in a sense, are partaking of the "corrupt fruit" of the devil.

Point out that we need to recognize the fruits of the devil so that we can avoid them. We also need to realize that we are judged by our own fruits. Other people around us see our deeds and actions and judge us. Throughout the scriptures we are told that Heavenly Father will ultimately judge us by our works, deeds, or "fruits."

Have someone read D&C 6:33. Explain to family members that we should never be afraid to do what is right. Heavenly Father watches us all the time and blesses us when we do good things.

ACTIVITY:

Remove any leftover cookies from the trees. Lay the apples with the words on them face down and allow family members to take turns choosing an apple and deciding which tree it belongs to, the "GOOD" or the "BAD."

Adorn the trees with the labeled apples and display them during the week. Place the apples without labels throughout the house and encourage family members to watch for other actions that could be added to the trees. When they notice one, have them write it on an apple and place it on the appropriate tree. Set a goal as a family to add more apples to the "GOOD" tree instead of to the "BAD" tree.

Handy Hint #5

On the Sunday before family home evening, ask one or two family members to read something interesting from a Church book or magazine. Have them give a report at the beginning of family home evening on what they've learned.

DECEPTION COOKIES

1 cup shortening (part butter or
    margarine)
1 ½ cups sugar
2 eggs
2 ¾ cups all-purpose flour

2 tsp. cream of tartar
1 tsp. soda
¼ tsp. salt
2 Tbsp. sugar
2 tsp. cinnamon

Heat oven to 400 degrees. Mix shortening, sugar, and eggs thoroughly. Measure flour by sifting. Blend flour, cream of tartar, soda, and salt, then stir into shortening mixture.

Reserve about ½ to ¾ cup dough and place in small bowl. Add enough extra **salt** to this small amount to make it taste awful. Shape this dough into 8-10 small balls, approximately ¾" in diameter. Roll these balls in a mixture of 2 tsp. **salt** and ½ tsp. cinnamon. Bake on ungreased cookie sheet for 8-10 minutes. Remove from oven and keep separate from the remaining cookies. Shape the remaining "good" dough into balls of the same size. Roll the balls in a mixture of 2 Tbsp. sugar and 2 tsp. cinnamon. Bake following the previous directions.

When cool, wrap the 8-10 **salty** cookies individually in plastic wrap. Secure with tape and attach them to one of the trees using tape or Fun-tack. Wrap about 3-4 of the good cookies the same way and fasten them to the other tree. These cookies may all look the same, but they certainly don't taste the same. Just ask my children!

Refer to the lesson for further instructions.

GOOD

BAD

"Heavenly Treasures"

"Lay up for yourselves a treasure in heaven, yea, which is eternal, and fadeth not away." Helaman 5:8

OBJECT:

To help us understand that we leave behind all earthly treasures when we die, while heavenly treasures are eternal—we keep them forever.

PREPARATION:

1. Copy, color, cut and laminate game board and pieces. Copy game board twice.
2. Assign the following scripture: Matthew 6:19-21

SUGGESTED SONG:

"I Need My Heavenly Father," Children's Songbook, p. 18.

LESSON:

Ask, "If you were going back to Heavenly Father today, what could you take with you?" Only heavenly treasures. Discuss what they are. Have someone read Matthew 6:19-21. Ask the meaning of the phrase, "where moth and rust corrupt, and where thieves break through and steal." Ask, "How many times have we bought something and then had it get old and break? Or how many times have we experienced theft in our lives?" It's comforting to know that all of our heavenly treasures can't "get old and break," nor can they be stolen! They are the only things we can take with us when we die.

Encourage family members to build up their heavenly treasures every day so that when they return to Heavenly Father, they will have many treasures.

To play the Heavenly Treasures game, begin by laying out the cards and the heavenly treasure coins and giving each team a game board. Tell your family they are going to play a game about actions that will help them earn heavenly treasures and about other actions that cause them to lose these treasures.

Divide your family into two teams. Lay all the cards facedown and all the coins faceup. Some of these cards are labeled with bad choices that result in losing a treasure. Other cards are labeled with good choices that result in earning a treasure. Some of these good choices are actually made while they are playing the game. Have the teams take turns drawing cards and doing what they say. If they fulfill the requirement on the card, they earn the appropriate coin. If they don't, the other team gets a chance to earn the coin by doing what the cards says. The first team that surrounds their heart with heavenly treasures wins the game.

Name three attributes of our Heavenly Father that you would like to work toward and earn the treasure of godliness.

You always try to think pure thoughts and dress modestly. You earn the treasure of chastity.

Sorry! You lose a treasure for boasting to your friends about all your new clothes.

Read Ephesians 4:32 and earn the treasure of tenderheartedness.

Whoops! You spent your tithing on candy. Give up one of your treasures.

You got upset with your parents because they wouldn't buy you an expensive pair of tennis shoes. Give up one of your treasures.

Oh-oh! You lied to your parents. Give up one of your treasures.

You chose to earn money on Sunday instead of going to church. Give up one of your treasures.

You cheated on a test so you could pass a class. Give up one of your treasures.

Whoops! You lost your temper and hit your little sister. Give up one of your treasures.

Sorry! Give up one of your treasures for spreading rumors about a friend.

Yipes! You watched too much TV and didn't allow time for scripture study. Give up one of your treasures.

Sorry! Give up one of your treasures for complaining about doing a church service project.

Rats! You didn't share your new toy with your little brother. Give up one of your treasures.

Oh-oh! You forgot to show your gratitude to your Heavenly Father. Give up one of your treasures.

Sing the song, "I Love to See the Temple," and earn the treasure of temple work.

Name three things you could do to bring someone into the church and earn the treasure of fellowshipping.

Name three things you would give away to help others and earn the treasure of charity.

Recite the 13th Article of Faith from memory and earn the treasures of chastity, benevolence, and virtue.

Read D&C 20:37 and earn the treasure of baptism.

Read Matthew 5:5 and 3 Nephi 12:5 and earn the treasure of meekness.

You study the scriptures daily and apply them in your daily life. You earn the treasure of wisdom.

You attend all of your church meetings and fulfill your church calling. You earn the treasure of dedication.

You have high standards that you firmly maintain. You earn the treasure of integrity.

You kneel down and bow your head when you pray. You earn the treasure of humility.

Explain why it's important to be trustworthy and earn its treasure.

You hear your friends saying bad things about someone you know. You tell them to stop and say good things about the person. You earn the treasure of loyalty.

You continue to invite your friends to church activities even though they have turned you down in the past. You earn the treasure of diligence.

Name three things you can do to be a dependable person and earn the treasure of dependability.

Name three things you can do to show respect for Heavenly Father and earn the treasure of respectfulness.

You quietly wait for your mother to get off the phone before speaking to her. You earn the treasure of patience.

You took care of a family member when they were sick. You earn the treasure of compassion.

Say something nice about a member of your family and earn the treasure of kindness.

Give the other team a free turn or one of your coins and earn the treasure of generosity.

You told the truth about something even though you knew you would get in trouble for it. You earn the treasure of honesty.

Your little sister hit you, but you didn't get mad at her. You earn the treasure of forgiveness.

Earn the treasure of love by giving someone a big hug and telling them that you love them.

You are striving to obey all the laws and ordinances of the gospel. You earn the treasure of righteousness.

Put a big smile on your face and earn the treasure of cheerfulness.

Explain the proper way to pray and earn the treasure of prayer.

Tell of three things you can do for someone else and earn the treasure of service.

Your friends were making fun of the church so you bore your testimony to them. You earn the treasure of courage.

Tell of something you are thankful for and earn the treasure of gratitude.

Read Moroni 4:10 and earn the treasure of faith.

Tell of a way you can be obedient to your parents and earn the treasure of obedience.

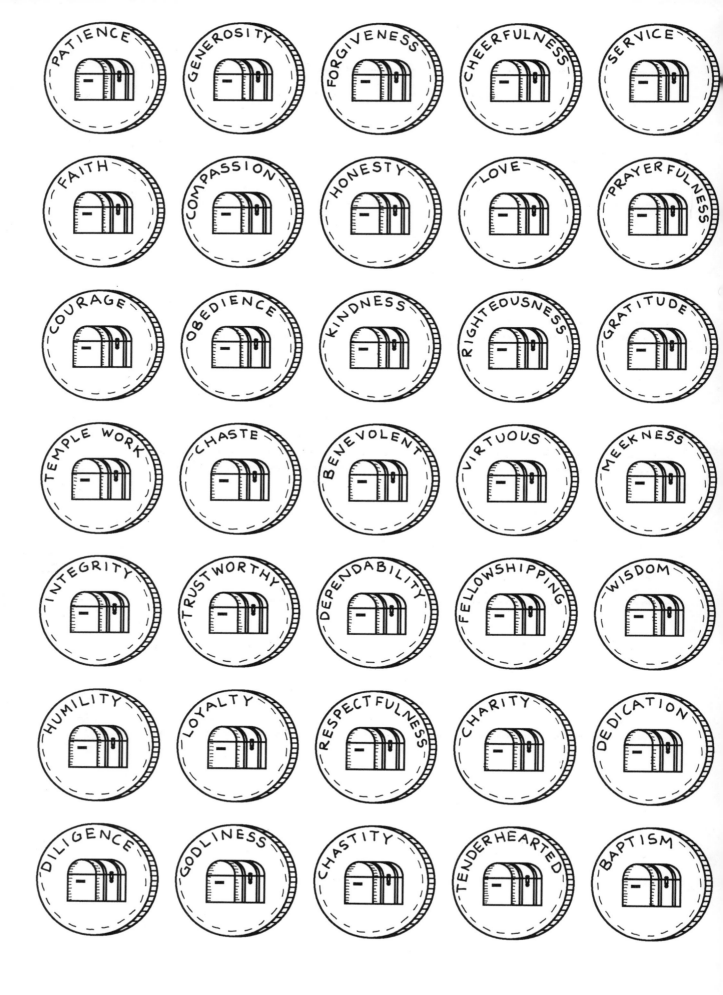

GAME BOARD

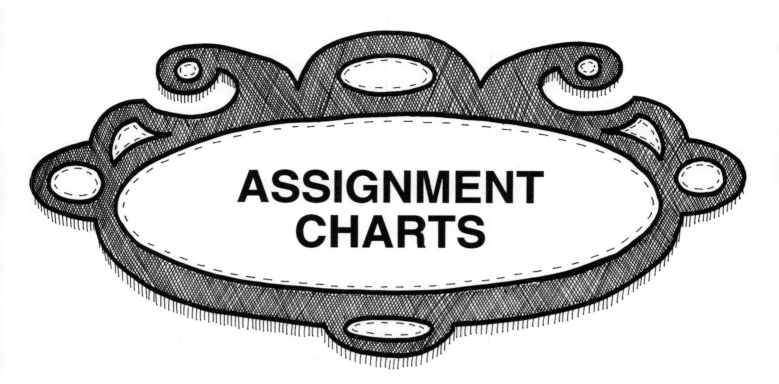

ASSIGNMENT
CHARTS

Country Window

Cut out one flower for each family member and write their name on it. Color the flowers and the window sill on page 66 with felt pens, crayons, colored pencils, etc. Laminate the various parts with clear contact paper or have them profession-ally laminated. Use "Fun-tack" to attach the flowers to the stems and rotate them each week.

Our family grows with
family home evening.

Sunshine

Cut out the face and the assignment circle. Write family names on the hearts of the sunshine on page 68. If there are not enough hearts for your family, team up older members with younger ones. Color the circles and the assignment chart and laminate them with clear contact paper or professional lamination. Place the face on top of the assignment circle then center both on the sunshine. Poke a paper brad through all the layers. Rotate the assignment wheel each week.

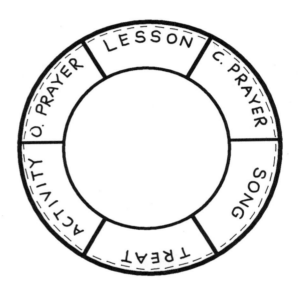

Handy Hint #6

Make a family suggestion box by decorating an old shoe box, jar, school box, etc. Encourage the family members to contribute their ideas and concerns to the suggestion box during the week. Address each contribution during the following family home evening.

OUR   FAMILY
SHINES BRIGHT
WITH
FAMILY HOME EVENING!